W. O. W

Moments

Moments of Worship Over Worry

Cornelius W. Dixon

W.O.W Moments

Printed in the United States of America

Copyright © 2016 Cornelius W. Dixon

First Printing:

ISBN-13:9781519139962

ISBN-10:1519139969

Kingdom Mandate Publications

Luverne AL, 36049

theauthorhimself@gmail.com

Contents

Introduction 5

Day 1 1

Day 2 3

Day 3 5

Day 4 7

Day 5 9

Day 6 11

Day 7 13

Day 8 15

Day 9 17

Day 10 19

Day 11 21

Day 12 23

Day 13 25

Day 14 27

Day 15 29

Day 16 31

Day 17 33

Day 18 35

Day 19 37

Day 20 39

Notes...41

Inspirational Message 81

Introduction

Every day brings about its own events. Some days are good, and some are bad. It is in those bad times where we need something to pick us up and give us strength throughout the day. Where else can we find the strength we need except in the word of God. Whatever you need you can find in the word of God. The joy, peace, and relief from the pressures of life can only be found in the word.

No matter the situation like throws your way, only way to deal with it is through worship and meditation on God's word. What you are facing now is only temporary, but God's word is eternal and able to sustain you in the midst of going through. No matter how many tears you cry! God will dry them. I know that many people are like me, have had so many sleepless nights, tossing and turning; pillow getting soaked with tears, but I hold fast to God's word that he will turn my mourning into dancing. We just have to wait for him.

I know we all have moments in life where situations occur and all we can say is "wow". Those times when your bills are more than your money, that is a wow moment. When you try your best to be the best person you can be, yet the conditions of life make it harder and harder to focus in life; that is a wow moment. Kids getting out of hand, marriage seems to be going down, seems like the odds of life are stacked against you and you can't

Find your way through; KNOW THAT GOD WILL DELIVER ON TIME!

Day 1
Against All Odds

Lord how they increase who trouble me! Many are they who rise up against me. Many are they who say of me, there is no help for him in God. But You, O Lord, are a shield for me, my glory and the one who lifts up my head.

Psalms 2: 1-3 (NKJV)

What do you do when you're facing life with the odds stacked against you? When the people around you seek to destroy you. When the things around you seem to be falling apart. We go through this life trying to advance and trying to find our way through the storm, yet we find ourselves facing problems. In those moments it seems as if the best thing to do is to give up and throw in the towel. I want to encourage you today to trust God even when the odds of life are stacked against you.

God is faithful and he is all powerful. He will see you through whatever you are facing. You just have to trust him; no matter the situations. Though you seem to be surrounded, yet he will make a way. Though you may find yourself broken, but God is able to mend together the broken pieces of

your life. When the enemy comes in to cause you to flip out Just remember that GOD IS YOUR SHEILD. He will protect you, though the enemy hits you with everything he has it won't harm you. Yes, you may feel it, yes it may seem to knock you down or shake you a little, but know that GOD WILL KEEP YOU!

So fear not my friend as to what the enemy tries to do, nor the people who come against you; because salvation belongs to God and his blessings is upon the righteous! When life throws a curve just Stand firm on the faith, trusting God against all odds.

Prayer:

Father in Jesus name I give you all the praises due your name. I honor you as the God of all and you are seated at the right hand of God making intercession for me. I ask you to help me in the times of trouble. I ask that you would cleanse me from all unrighteousness of actions and conversations. Cover me in your blood and protect me in with your powerful hand. In Jesus name, Amen!

Day 2
Don't Lose Hope

for the law made nothing perfect; on the other hand, there is the bringing in of a better hope, through which we draw near to God.

Hebrews 7:19(NKJV)

I remember talking to a friend of mine about a dream she had that really struck with me. In the dream my friend Sam took her dog Prosperity out to use the bathroom outside. While Prosperity was walking in the yard, Sam's friend Hope came up and the began to converse with each other. Sam noticed prosperity began to stray away and she turned to retrieve prosperity and upon getting her closer to her she looked up and saw hope walking away. The further away hope got away the darker it became. All a sudden hope was out of Sam's sight and a storm came. Thunder, lightning, and rain began to display. Sam grabbed Prosperity and began to walk to the house. When she got to the stairs leading to the door with every step she took her feet began to get heavy until she just could not make it any further. She called for her mother and there was nothing she could do.

In life don't lose sight of hope trying to focus on other things and people. There is nothing wrong with having prosperity, but prosperity won't help you in the times of storms. Don't allow the people and possessions in your life to be a hindrance from joy, love, and peace in your life.

Life is full of transitional periods that consist of good and bad times, therefore you should build your hopes on the things that last. Let your hope be based on the things of the spirit. Not in the materialistic things in which prosperity bring, let it be in the one who makes prosperity possible; the Lord God!

Prayer:

Father in Jesus name I praise you O Lord. You are my strength, my joy and the hope of my life. I ask you to help me to remember you in the times of my life, good and bad. Help me to experience joy and peace in the midst of my storms. Give me hope and keep me from losing happiness in times of trouble. I trust you and I ask that you keep me in your loving arms. In Jesus name, Amen.

And above all things have fervent love for one another, for "love will cover a multitude of sins."

1Peter 4:8(NKJV)

ove is a powerful tool, and an important characteristic to have. Without love we not only become bound, but we bind those around us. I don't care how much money you have; how many degrees you have or what your status is in life; without love you are still have nothing.

Love surpasses an emotional feeling; it is an expression of action that manifests a characteristic. Love is not what you feel it is what you do because of who you are. If you sing you are considered to be a singer. The same with love, if you have love then you operate in love because that's who you are.

The characteristics of love is being able to love those who hate you. It is being able to willfully help those who are desires to see you struggle. Love has the power to change the lives of your enemies. If you love God and you are a child of the King, you therefore must operate in this type of love. The agape love, the unconditional love of Christ must be the drive that causes you to love and thus you can be loved.

Love in spite of what others say and do towards you. Proverbs 10:12 also teaches us "Hatred stirs up strife, but love covers all sins." (NKJV). When you decided to love others in spite of their actions toward you, God will be glorified and he will step in on your behalf. Failure to show love only makes things worse. When you see someone you know don't like you; speak to them, bless them, pray for them to be blessed. Don't allow people the power to command your day! You stand up in love and walk in the authority that God has given you!

Prayer:

Father in Jesus name I ask that you would help me to love unconditionally. Fill me with your love to display to all that I come in contact with in my everyday life. Help me not to allow my emotions and anger to hinder me from showing love, even when someone does wrong to me. Bless my enemies, and watch over those who come to cause me to fall! Give me the strength and the passion to overcome in Jesus name I pray, Amen!

Day 4
Yet Will I Trust Him

Though He slay me, yet will I trust him.

Job 13:15(NKJV)

*L*ife has a way of throwing unexpected curves your way. Things can be going good for you one day and you're struggling the next. Your health is fair today, but poor tomorrow. Your family is doing fine this minuet then in an instance someone has died or has been in some harmful situation. It seems like when one thing comes it's usually followed by a series of other circumstances, and it seems as if life it's self comes to destroy you!

Those sleepless nights, where you tossed and turned all night, crying and praying to hear from God. Pillow soak and wet with tears, I want to encourage you and let you know; it is not in vain. God has seen your struggle, he has counted your tears, he has kept note of the countless hours you have spent in tears. He is our high priest and he can be touched with the feelings of our infirmities. He is asking you today, will you just trust me in the midst of the opposition in life. God allows us to go through not only to bring him the glory, but to also bless you and show you just how strong you really are! The hardest battles are always given to the strongest soldiers!

Just like Job. He was a great man with a great life until one-day destruction seemed to bully his life. He lost his children, his livelihood, he became sick, his friends turned on him and his wife seem to have lost his mind. In the midst of all this going on in Job's life he never sinned nor did he accuse God of wrong.

Though he experienced some emotional moments, yet in the midst of that Job decided to Worship Over Worry!

Remember this very vital thing, the very things you are facing right now will not even be an issue in the time to come. Though it may hurt and may be hard right now, AFTER THIS you will see just how blessed you really are!

Prayer:

Father in Jesus name, I ask that you help me to become more like your servant Job. Help me to trust you in times of victory and in times of struggle. Father help me to keep my eyes focused on you, and keep my trust in you that I may not see defeat in my situation, but that I see victory in the midst of my battles. Help me to praise you like the battle is over, even when I'm still fighting. I understand that my praise and trust in you is the greatest weapons in which I can fight with! Amen.

Day 5
Praise Break at Midnight

But at midnight Paul and Silas were praying and singing hymns to God...suddenly there was a great earthquake, so that the foundations of the prison were shaken; and immediately all the doors were open and everyone's chains were loosed.

Acts 16:25,26(NKJV)

o you have a midnight praise? Midnight is the time of night, that begins a brand new day. It is determined that midnight is the darkest part of the night. That's a great rejoicing point simply because even though you see the darkness from the previous day, yet you're in a whole new day. It's another day for God to show up in your situation, another opportunity for him to manifest himself too you!

Praising God in the midst of your midnight experience in life will do two things: when Paul and Silas praised God in the midst of their midnight, the bible said that a great earthquake came and 1. Doors were open... Your midnight praise can open doors your enemy have shut. 2. everyone's chains were loosed... The praise you give God can deliver you from the thing that seem to be holding you captive, not only you but those around you. Do you have a midnight praise?

Even though it may be dark right now, just praise Him. Know this that the darkest hour is just before the breaking of day. With a new day comes new mercies, and renewed compassion from God. The darkest part of the tunnel is right in the middle, just keep moving. Don't allow the darkness to make you stationary, waiting for light to come; realize that if you have

Jesus then you have the light. God's word is a lamp to your feet and a light to your path. Your steps have already been ordered by him, just keep going!

Prayer:

Father in Jesus name, I pray that you help me to continue to praise you in the midst of midnight in my life. Give me the attitude of David, to bless you at all times and continuously praise you with the fruit of my lips. I ask you to help me to give you a permanent praise through the temporary situations of life's midnight. I thank you in advance for the new day that I am coming into! In Jesus Name, Amen!

Day 6
Employing the struggle

and we know all things work together for good to those who love God, to those who are the called according to His purpose.

Romans 8:28(NKJV)

*L*earn how to employ the struggles of your life. What I mean is; learn how to make the things you face in life to work to your advantage. You are the employer and your struggle is the employee. Though the struggle may seem to be benefiting; all in all; it's working to make your life better. If I were a business owner, I would hire employees that will make my business more successful and that's the mindset we should have with our struggles in life. When you enter a struggle, don't begin to fear but take authority over it and cause it to work for your good.

James chapter two we learn how the trials of life benefits us as Christians. Though they come and seem to utterly destroy us, but it is working on the inside something far more valuable than what we can see from the natural eyes. Your struggle comes with a purpose, and failure to hang on in the midst of the struggle causes you to forfeit all that God is trying to do for you, to you, and through you!

So when you face any type of struggle in your life, you should remember that God is turning it around for you! That thing the enemy thought would destroy you, God will use to establish you! Keep your head up, don't give up; nor throw in the towel! You may have to cry sometimes, but know that God will turn it around for your good. You may have to give up something in your life, but God will turn it around for your good. Friends and family may turn their backs on you, but God will turn it around for your good! So hold your head up high, square your shoulder, and continue to press your way through the struggle!

Prayer:

Father in Jesus name I thank you for the trials in my life. Though times are hard, and times I can 't see you near, I know that you are there. I thank you for the trials that you allow into my life, for the purpose of building me and strengthening me. Give me the ability to remain faithful until you have brought me out of this situation. I give you glory, honor, and praise in advance, and I trust you against all odds, in Jesus name; Amen!

Day 7
The Pull of Purpose

Now my soul is troubled, and what shall I say? "Father save me from this hour"? But for this purpose I came to this hour. Father, glorify your name.

Matthew 13:27-28(NKJV)

*I*n my first book; "Reaching Beyond the Break", I shared with the readers a revelation of an ordinary rope. How it is made, how it breaks, and the purpose (purposes) that it is used. The rope represents our life in all that it contains. It is symbolic of the pain, the process and the obstacles in which we face. The rope has to be connected to God, in order for it to be connected to our purpose. Therefore, when the process begins to push us out, purpose can draw us back in.

This is why you can't give up in situations that you feel like throwing in the towel, simply because purpose keeps on pulling you! This thing may be hard right now, and you just want to give up and go another route, but purpose keeps on pulling you. Yes, you may have to cry sometimes, but purpose keeps on pulling. Though there is a struggle going on in your spirit, and it seem like you're at the door to destruction, but purpose will not allow you to become defeated.

There is a purpose to every situation! The only way to allow purpose to have full control is to divorce your feelings and embrace the will of God. Even Jesus wanted to give up in times of trial as he prepared to go to the cross. Remember he prayed father let this cup pass from me, but never the less that God's will be done.

There are times in my life where I wanted to just go the other way, but purpose kept pulling me. I wanted to lose my mind, and do the things I wanted to do; but purpose kept pulling me. Though I have strayed sometimes, but I couldn't stay because my purpose was stronger than my struggle and it just kept on pulling me. I had to learn not to pity my situation, but to glorify God; because my purpose was being constructed. Understand this, your purpose is always bigger than you!

Prayer:

Father, in Jesus name; I thank you for the trials and struggles of my life. I ask God that you will help me to change the things I can and give me the strength to trust you with the things I have no control over. Help me to not give up but accept the things you allow into my life. I ask that you be glorified in my life and all situations that I encounter. I thank you for purpose, and the process in Jesus Name AMEN!

Day 8

Greater is Coming

For I consider the sufferings of this present time are not worthy to compare to the glory which shall be revealed in us.

Romans 8:18(NKJV)

Have you ever experienced trials in your life that seem to vex you? You try everything in your power to pray for better days, but there is no strength or hope for tomorrow in sight. I encourage you to hang on in there, simply because your greater is coming! No matter what it looks like, feel like or sound like, your greater is on the way!

The things you face right now may be hard, but where you are right now, is only preparation for what is to come. The tears you cry today only prepares you for the joy that is to come. The pain you experience now only prepares you for the relief that comes tomorrow. Do not continue to dwell on the right now to where you forget or ignore the fact that right now will someday become an after this! Things are going to better! When you step in to your "after this" season, you will see that the struggle was all worth it! In order for you to reach the next level of your life, you have to go through somethings. When you're in school you have to complete exams in order to graduate to the next level. With each level the test may seem harder, but it's not impossible. God is only preparing you!

Find strength and comfort in knowing that God has delivered you before and will do it again. I don't care what your situation is, it is never too hard for God. There are no limits to what God can do for you. Trust Him and let Him handle it. Praise Him as if He's already done it. Keep praising Him until he brings you out.

Prayer:

Father in Jesus name, I thank you for the trials I face in my life. They are to make me strong. Help me to continue to faithfully serve you and praise you until I pass the test. I thank you for being a keeper and a present help. I ask you to give me the strength for today and the faith for tomorrow. I give you glory, I give you honor, and I give you praise for the glory which is to come. I call on your name today, because of the great power that resides in your name. For your name is higher than every name, and at the sound of your name troubles will have to cease. For there is no other name given by which all men can be saved. It is in that most high name of Jesus I pray, Amen!

Day 9
Make Me over

And the vessel made of clay was marred in the hand of the potter; so he made it again into another vessel, as it seemed good to the potter to make.

Jeremiah 18:4 (NKJV)

Keep your head up! Only time you should have your head down, is when you are finding the broken pieces of your life as you pick them up; preparing to take them to the potter to reshape and remold you! The Potter master's in the reconstruction of the vessels that have been broken by the conditions of life. What a great experience and privilege to be shaped at the hands of the potter. Through all of our imperfections and flaws that comes in our lives, the potter is ready willing and able to put us back together again!

God is the potter and you're the clay. If you will submit your being to Him and allow Him to build you and shape you, there will be greatness to come to you. Though it may not be an easy process being turned and shaped; in the end you will experience the glory. Though God may have to scrape some things off of you, and dig some things out of you, the finished product will be held in honor by the potter!

A potter has many vessels that it has made. There is a thing that the potter calls a "Chosen Vessel". The chosen vessel is not always displayed in the public's eye. The chosen vessel is often times isolated from all the others awaiting special occasions for the potter to bring them out to show forth the glory and works of his hands. You may be feeling as if you're isolated and put on the back shelf, but God is saying it's because you're chosen. You may feel like you can't fit in with others, and no one recognizes the beauty you contain, but it's only because you're chosen. Don't allow the popularity of others intimidate you and cause you to feel worthless!

God will take all the bitterness, all the pain, all the hard times. He'll take all of the brokenness and imperfections and mix them to bring forth a beautiful vessel of honor. That which your enemies have used for your destruction, God will use for your elevation! And he will make you into something that He sees as good!

Prayer:

Father in Jesus Name I ask you to take me through your making process! Change me, heal me and create me into a vessel of honor for your glory. I want to be like you; to live for you! Create in me a clean heart, and renew the right spirit with in me. I know your hands are capable of putting together my brokenness! In Jesus Name I pray; Amen!

Day 10
Don't Lose your Head

and do not be conformed to this world, but be transformed by the renewing of your mind, that you may prove what is that good and acceptable and perfect will of God.

Romans 12:2 (NKJV)

The struggles of life, the chaos that seems to come with every day, the residue of the past all mixed with doubt or fear of your future can be overwhelming. Don't fret, don't be dismayed; for this is not the time to lose your head! Let this be the last day you allow yourself to become bent out of shape because of what seems to be a painful or stressful season of your life. Keep your mind on God and remember that things will not always be like this.

Why is it so important to keep your mind? The bible teaches that God will keep you in perfect peace if your mind is set and focused on Him (Isaiah 26:3). Not your problems, not your bills, not your sickness or whatever the situations are, you have to keep your mind stayed on him. If the enemy can take over your mind with the burdens of your life, he's got you right where he wants you. The enemy will cause you to focus so much on your pain, to where you neglect to remember what God has already promised you through his word. You have to keep your head!

If it wasn't important to keep your head, why then would Paul have said as you take upon yourself the whole armor of God, to take on the helmet of salvation? Because, the helmet is what is going to protect your head. If it wasn't important, why then would Paul have also said for you to be transformed in the renewing of your mind. If your mind is stuck on defeat, how then can you walk in victory? Be encouraged and keep your mind focused on God. Though it may be hard right now, but things are going to get better. Just trust God!!

Prayer:

Father in Jesus name, I ask you to touch my heart and my mind. Bring me into deeper understanding and encourage me. Minister to me in the midst of the struggle, and help me to hold on until you bring me through these trials. Father I submit my all to you, lead me and guide me. I trust you and I ask that you give me peace in the midst of the storms. By Faith I praise you in the midst of my storm as if I am out of the storm. I praise you in advance for the victory that is to come. In Jesus Name, Amen!

Day 11

You're not in this alone

Yea, though I walk through the valley of the shadow of death, I will fear no evil; For You are with me; Your rod and Your staff, they comfort me.

Psalms 23:4(NKJV)

I think one of the most common side effects of the struggle is thinking you are in this all by yourself. Seems like no one or understands or even care to comprehend what it is you're going through. There are times in our lives where we feel or have felt completely alone! I want to let you know today that; you are not alone! For God is with you through every situation you face. Even though sometimes you may not be able to feel him, sometimes you may not be able to hear him, but know that he is still there. He will not leave you, neither will he abandon you!

Even in the face of death, know that God is right there with you! To guide you, he's there to protect you and strengthen you! Don't allow the condition of your surroundings, blind you! You have to look beyond what you see in the natural eye, and hold fast to what you see in the spirit. Through the sleepless nights, God is there! He sees you tossing and turning, He hears you crying, and He is there to comfort you. It's awesome to serve a God who never sleeps nor slumbers, but he's always standing by, making intersession for us to the father!

Keep your head up, be not dismayed, knowing that God is standing right beside you. Just talk to him, things will get better. He will show you the right way to God, just trust him, even when you can't trace him!

Prayer:

Father I thank you for never leaving me. I thank you for never giving up on me in the times of struggle. I ask dear father that you strengthen me, and keep me. Help me to walk through the valley, and bring me out unharmed! You are my protector, and I need you to bring me through that I may be there for someone else in their times of need. In Jesus Name I pray, Amen!

Day 12

Just move forward

And the Lord said to Moses, "Why do you cry to me? Tell the children of Israel to go forward"

Exodus 14:15(NKJV)

I think a lot of times we become so overwhelmed by the things that have transpired, that we fail to realize we have to move on. We become stuck in the emotional trauma of the temporary situation, that we fail to realize it was only temporary! Yes, we may still experience some after effects and still see some residue from the struggle, but we have to keep our focus on overcoming the struggles.

No matter what your struggle was, there is life beyond the wrestling. You may find yourself in Moses' place, with the children of Israel; stuck between the bondage you come out of and the sea blocking you from obtaining the promises of God. Don't spend too much crying about what it looks like, based on the emotions of the moment. Pick yourself up and move on. You have been in this place to long, and the only way to come out and move on to promise, is by moving forward, knowing that God is going to be by your side through the entire journey. Move forward looking to the victory that awaits. Nothing in your past is worth taking with you, if it were; God would have anointed it to come with you. You just have to move forward. Though you may have to leave some family, may have to walk away from some friends, may have to give up something in your life; it is important that you let go and move on! The most dangerous place you can be in this season of your life is a place of no progression. You have to move forward to advance to the next level in your life!

Prayer:

Father in Jesus name, I give you glory, honor, and praise! Thank you for delivering me and setting me free from the bondage that held me captive. Now God I ask you to strengthen me, and help me to move forward in the life you have pre-ordained me to live. I ask that you give me the wisdom and guidance to walk in the steps in which you have ordered for me. With every step I make, Lord I give you the glory. In Jesus name, Amen!

Day 13
Awake Arise & Conquer

...Breath came into them, and they lived, and stood upon their feet, and exceedingly great army.

Ezekiel 37:10(NKJV)

Have you found yourself in a place of hopelessness or despair? You come to the point where you're all dried out and have no power to live; neither desire to stand. You've become content with the mindset that life will not get better, so you lay there in your struggle. It's time for you to get up! Awake, Arise, and Conquer! This is not the time to lose your mind or have pity party. God has summons you to arise in him, that he may show forth his glory to you! No matter where you are in life, and no matter how you got there; the important thing for you to realize is that you do not have to stay there; for God has planted the spirit of a solider in you! Stand up and fight!

How awesome is it to know that God did not forget about you in the midst of your struggle! Even though we are our worse enemies at times, his grace and mercy has kept us; even in our unfaithfulness. Do not allow your current situations cause you to lay unresponsive! Get up, dust yourself off and continue to fight until you overcome your situation! You have to realize that the victory has already been won, and the battle which you face is not yours to fight. All God wants you to do is be present at the battle. Only way you need to fight is by praising God! When Jehoshaphat went to battle against the people of Moab, Ammnon and Mt. Sier; he sent out the praise team before the army. The bible says that at the time of the battle, the people began to praise God and God set up an ambush against their enemy! Your praise is your weapon. You can conquer this! When the devil tries to darken your day, don't fret; Just praise. Praise will help you though every situation you have ever faced and ever will face! Awake, Arise, & Conquer; by realizing, things will get better. Just praise God like its already done!

Prayer:

Father in Jesus Name, Lord I thank you for your goodness and your mercy. I praise you for your wonderful and awesome power. I realize God that you are in control of all things. I ask that you help me to conquer the situations I face in life that seem tare me apart. Help me to awake, arise, & conquer. Breathe into me the breath of life, that I may stand a living vessel for your glory! Take me higher in you, and in your word. I praise you even in the midst of opposition in my life. To you be all glory, honor, and praise; In Jesus Name, Amen!

Day 14
Overcoming The World!

These things I have spoken to you, that in Me you may have peace. In the world you will have tribulation; but be of good cheer, I have overcome the world.

John 16:33(NKJV)

In life you will find that there are many trials and tribulation that you will face. When it rains, it pours. Seems like you can experience a good season that ultimately turns in to the worst season you've experienced. Life has a way of throwing unexpected changing in your midst. There's good news, you don't have to fret, the troubles you face right now, Won't last always!

The things you experience in life are but temporal situations, but the build in you eternal characteristics. The storms of the life only cause you to become fertile and able to bear fruit. The trying of your faith builds patience, and hope, on the inside. Though you may see chaos, there is greatness being created behind the scene.

Don't waste your time trying to fight against what the world has thrown your way. Why because Jesus Christ has already overcome the word. He told us that in the world you will have hard times, but be of good cheer, simply because HE has already won the victory on your behalf! No matter what it may seem like, no matter how it may feel; God has already worked it out on your behalf. Realize that the victory is already in you, because Jesus is in you! Greater is he that is within you than he that is within the world.

Prayer:

Father I thank you for the sacrifice you made for me through Christ Jesus! Give me the power and the strength to stand in the midst of the tribulation of life. I ask that you would keep me grounded in your word. I thank you for peace even in the midst of chaos, knowing that after I have suffered a little while; you oh Lord, the God of all peace will strengthen me and bring me out better than ever before. I give you praise, honor and glory in Jesus name; Amen!

Day 15
Daddy's Hands

Though I walk in the midst of trouble, You will revive me; You will stretch out Your hand against the wrath of my enemies, and Your right hand will save me.

Psalms 138:7(NKJV)

*P*aul teaches us in 1 Peter 5 the importance of casting away your cares. The things that seem to be a great concern to you. Those things in which you're easily worried or moved by emotionally, physically, and spiritually. He teaches you to cast it all to the Lord, because God cares about you. He cares about everything, be it big or small; God cares about all things concerning you! No matter what you're facing in your current situation; God cares about it. He cares so much so, to where the very hairs on your head is numbered. That alone is a great reason to give your all over to the Lord.

Giving your situations over to God means that it's no longer a burden to you; It's in the best place it can be, The hands of the Almighty God. The Problem is a lot of times we take our problems to God and we ask him to fix them, yet we always seem to take them back and continue to worry. When you take your burdens to the Lord, you have to leave them there and allow him to work it out in due time. If you would just position yourself under the hand of the almighty; you will then find that everything you need is in the presence of the Lord.

Why is it so important to have your life and the situations that come with it? Because it is under God's hand where you find the will of God for your life, healing for the wounds you have, and the protection from the danger that lies awaiting the opportunity to take you out! He's able to handle your every circumstance!

My friend Sam shared with me a situation she experienced riding down the road on afternoon. She saw a man and his daughter by the roadside, their car had broken down. Samantha observed the man as his daughter waited on the sidewalk beside the care, patiently waiting. As her dad came around to her, she reached up; placing her hand in his hand. She didn't move until her father moved. She followed the direction of her father. Why was that so amazing to her" Because the fact that the little girl trusted her father so much so, that even in the midst of a "break down"; she knew that daddy was there to protect and cover her. No matter what your situation is; in daddy's hands; you can make it through the storms of life. Even when it seems as if you're all alone, know that God is still there; He's just simply carrying you through the storm!

Prayer:

Father in Jesus name, thank you for another day. I realize that my life and all the struggles that may come with it, is all in your hands. Thank you for guiding me, strengthening me, and covering me with your mighty hand. Father I trust you to bring me through the storm; and in the moment of my weakness, thank you for carrying me through the storms! I give you glory, honor, and praise; for being the awesome God you are. In Jesus Name, Amen!

Day 16
God is Able

If that is the case, our God whom we serve is able to deliver us from the burning fiery furnace, and He will deliver us from your hand O king!

Daniel 3:17(NKJV)

I have heard this saying several times in my walk with God, and it wasn't until recently I gained full understanding of what is being said; and that is the quote, "If you don't stand for something, you will fall for anything!" This saying is very true. In life, more specifically; a Christian life, we are to live by the standards of holiness; compromising nothing. If it's in the word, we are to live by the word. It is the only way to receive the promises and protection of God. We have to be careful not to allow man made laws push us to walk contrary to God's word, regardless of what man may threaten to do, how society may look at you, you have to stand up for what is right, and uphold the standards of holiness. There is a reason the root word of standard is stand.

Through the trials, battles, and opposition in life; you've got to continue to stand. Having taken all the necessary preparations, when you've done all you can do; continue to stand firm; knowing that God is able to do everything but fail. I know that seems easier said than done. I look at the story of the three Hebrew boys, facing the king and I had to ask myself "Am I willing to stand for God, even when my life is on the line?". You must be willing to continue to stand, even when it's not popular to stand. When people decide to look at you crazy. Knowing that God is ready, willing, and able to deliver you. Even if he doesn't step in it doesn't mean he's not able. We got to realize we can't "Quid-Pro-Quoi" God. God I will stand for you if you do this for me. If the truth be told, he's already done more than enough for us; even when we were undeserving of it he still has shown his love for us!

Even in the midst of your standing, it may push you into a greater level of testing, but don't worry; God is just showing you that HE IS ABLE! You know this story. The king had the three Hebrew boys thrown into the furnace and it was heated seven times hotter than normal. They were shackled and bound. King came back, saw them walking in the midst of the fire, here's where God really showed out. The king asked "did we not throw three into the fire, then why do I see four; and the fourth one looks like the Son of God!" Let me drop this for you like this. This is an old testament scripture; Jesus was not physically here until the new testament; How can the king say what Jesus look like; if in fact he has never seen Him! I want you to know that I don't care what has happened to you, or maybe happening right now, or will happen in the future. Stand and know that God is able, and that when God steps into your situation; those who threw you in the fire will know that the divine hand of God is over your life! When he brings you out, you won't look like what you been through! Remind yourself every day that GOD IS ABLE!

Prayer:

Father in Jesus name I praise you! You are the almighty sovereign God, and I thank you Lord that you are able to do exceedingly and abundantly above all I can ask or think. Help me God to stand for you, and trust you in the midst of opposition in my life! I thank you God that in my times of weakness, that you remain strong. Strengthen me God, and keep your hand on me. I give you the glory, the honor and praise! In Jesus Name, Amen!

Day 17
Take A Selfie

Now therefore, thus says the Lord of hosts: "Consider your ways! You have sown so much, and bring in little; You eat, but do not have enough; You drink, but you are not filled with drink; You clothe yourselves, but no one is warm; And he who earns wages, earns wages to put into a bag with holes."

Haggai 1:5-6(NKJV)

I think this is one of the most difficult actions one is to take; but it is very important. Let's face it, every struggle we face or have faced in life is not always because of other people or random occurrence; somethings are indeed manifested struggle through our own sinful desires and ignorance. It is a part of our fleshly character. A lot of times in the storm we have to sit back and reflect, and ask ourselves "Why am I here?" We sometimes try and point the blame everywhere, when a lot of times we should just look in the mirror. If the truth be told, we can be our own worst enemy. Satan don't have to beat us with anything, because we're too busy beating up ourselves.

You are not a bad person because of mistakes you've made in your life. You do not have to stay in this place you are at, first step to coming out is looking at yourself deeply within and finding what may have gone wrong to push you into this place; and when you've found it acknowledge it exists; and let God help you! You have to be real with yourself and be real with God. Yes, take a selfie. Unfiltered and unedited. So that you can see the flaws and the things out of balance, that way you can take them to God and deal with them. Let's not be so quick to want a release from God; when we are still in denial about the struggles we are bound by.

Don't find yourself living the rest of your life in the shoes of the people of Judah. God has so much he wants for you and from you. Yet you take care of your own selves more than you seek for him. Thus you find yourself in lack and in despair, why? Because you're not focusing. Don't be so busy to build yourself up in the finer things in life and forget about the Kingdom. You so built up in the house, yet your life is a mess. Your so caught up in the money, yet your prayer life and dedication to God's word is in a mess. Failure to operate in the will of God will always result in a drought. You can make six figures, yet if you're not in his will; you have nothing. You can be the biggest giver in the house, but if you're not in his will, there is little to no harvest. Only way to fix this type of thing is to take self-inventory; and find the things of your life that have expired and you still trying to hold on to; and let it (or them) GO!

Prayer:

Father in Jesus name I thank you for the life you have blessed me to live. Help me everyday father to do things that will be uplifting in building your kingdom. Lord I ask that you examine me, and show me the real me. Everything that is not like you or beneficial to the life you have called me to live, take it out. Deliver me, and help me to be the person you have called me to be. That as I live according to your will, that the blessings and favor of God will consume my life. That the seeds I sow will be multiplied and not devoured. That I have more than enough spiritually and physically, that you cover me in all I do according to your will for me. I give you praise, honor and glory in Jesus name, Amen!

Day 18
Sun Stand Still - keep fighting

And the sun stood still, and the moon stayed, until the people had avenged themselves upon their enemies...

Joshua 10:13(KJV)

*L*et me go directly to the point, God will cause a supernatural stand still, until you overcome the struggle you face! What a great and awesome God we serve, that he would not allow a new day to come with the present day ending in the defeat of his people. Be encouraged in the fact that this day is not a day of defeat for you, if you're trusting in God it is a day of great victory and triumph!

No matter how long you have to fight, keep fighting. No matter how many people walk away from you, no matter what you have to give up; remember that the SON will not go away. In this text the sun continued to shine until Joshua and the people were victorious; but for you I want you to know that the S.O.N will continue to shine for you until you have overcome your situation! I know the battle seems to be hard, I know at times it seems that defeat is about to overtake you; but as long as the SON is shining, that just simply means that there is still a chance for you to reign in victory!

God is surely there fighting for you, fighting with you, fighting through you! No matter how many things come up against you, you plus God equals the majority. No matter who comes up to fight against you, remember that HE that abides in you is much greater than he that abides in the world. Declare to yourself "This day there will be victory in my life!" Victory in your home, Victory on your job, Victory in your finances! No darkness can over take the shine of the sun!

Prayer:

Father in Jesus name, that name which is higher than every other name. I praise your wonderful name! I thank you Jesus that you will not allow me to die in defeat, but that you stand beside me and fight with me that I may live in victory! I honor you almighty God! For you are a great and awesome God, you are a strong and mighty God, Mighty in battle. Thank you for the victory you have already won, I just ask you continue to strengthen me where I am weak, that I may be able to stand in the midst of the battle until the victory is manifested in my life. I give you glory, I give you honor, and I give you praise. In Jesus Name! Amen

Day 19
It Won't Always Be Like This

After you have suffered for a little while, the God of all grace [who imparts His blessing and favor], who called you to His own eternal glory in Christ, will Himself complete, confirm, strengthen, and establish you [making you what you ought to be].

1 Peter 5:10(AMP)

Look at yourself in the mirror and remind yourself everyday "It won't always be like this!" It's not a matter of "If" things get better, you have to know and declare that things WILL get better, and they are already turning around for your good. The Lord will do it sooner than you think, and when God brings you out you will be even more greater than you went it. There will be a greater anointing, more joy, more love, more peace! Just wait on it, because it is surely coming to you! You may be experiencing some lack, but God will deliver you into abundance!

I want you to remember that you cannot humanly comprehend God and why he does the things the way he does, all you can do is trust him and know that he has a purpose! Though it may hurt right now, but that only makes you appreciate the peace that is to come later. At the end of the struggle you see what you went through did not take you out, but it pushed you into your blessed place! I think that is a great place to give God a mighty praise, because of what is to come! Knowing that there is a greater glory that comes after the struggle is the greatest encouragement one can ask for! You won't be here too long. God knows just when to put you in and when to bring you out!

The text said AFTER you have suffered a little while. You got to understand first of all God did not bring you into the struggle to stop right there! He didn't allow trouble to enter your life in order to put a period there; instead he put a comma, letting you know take a deep breath something greater than this is coming your way! After you have struggled a little while, THEN THE GOD OF PEACE SHALL complete, confirm, strengthen, and establish you! In other word's God will use your struggle to birth you into the person and place that he pre-ordained you to be! Tell yourself "My struggle is making me!"

Hold your head up! Stick your chest out! And know that even though it may be dark right now, but the darkest hour is right before the breaking of day! It won't always be like this!

Prayer:

Father in the mighty name of Jesus, I thank you for a turnaround in my situation. I thank you God for not allowing my trials to take me out, but to actually give me greater in life. I thank you for the struggle, that you may get the glory from my deliverance. Father I trust you, I walk in the steps you have ordered for me, and I give you all praise in advance for the shift that is about to take place! I love you Jesus, I magnify you in my situation. I make you bigger than my circumstances! Have your way, and let your will be done; in Jesus name I pray, AMEN!

Day 20
I'm coming out of this!

Therefore, we do not become discouraged [spiritless, disappointed, or afraid]. Though our outer self is [progressively] wasting away, yet our inner self is being [progressively] renewed day by day. For our momentary, light distress [this passing trouble] is producing for us an eternal weight of glory [a fullness] beyond all measure [surpassing all comparisons, a transcendent splendor and an endless blessedness]!

2 Corinthians 4:16-17(AMP)

I want you to know and understand, God can and will take your situation and use it for his glory! Remember the very same God who raised Jesus from the dead is the exact same God who is working in your struggles and will also raise you up! Therefore, do not allow what it looks like or feels like to burden you and make you lose sight of what God is doing for you! For the struggled you face are only temporary, and there is an expiration date! You are not going to go through this for the rest of your life! So even though you may be down, you're not knocked out. Though you may be perplexed! God is about to do something miraculous in your situation! And it's not just for you, but also it's for the benefit of the doubters that they might believe!

This not the time to question God or give up and throw in the towel. You have got to hang on in there and go through, for God is about to work this thing out and YOURE COMING OUT! Don't hurry your storm, because it's working for you a more eternal and exceeding weight of glory! Just believe in your God! He is there through it all. He's holding you in the hard times. He takes account of every tear that you cry in those sleepless nights. The God of Israel is not ignorant of the things you face, for he never slumbers nor sleeps, but his eyes are always open and his ear attentive unto the cries of his people. He is mending your brokenness, He is healing your every illness, he is supplying your every need! For HE is God and beside him there is no other, LET GOD WORK, You're coming out! Don't just come out, come out with a great and mighty shout! Come out with your hands up, lifting up the name of Jesus!!

Prayer:

Father I thank you for deliverance. I thank you for the glory that comes after the struggle. For you oh God is worthy of all the glory, honor and praise. You are great and sovereign. I trust you oh God for your ways are not like my ways, and your thoughts are higher than my thoughts. I praise you in advance for what you are about to do in my situation in life. You are great, and greatly to be praised! So Father be magnified in my life, be glorified in my life! I honor you, My God, My King! Continue to complete, perfect, establish, and strengthen me! I give you the highest praise, in the great and mighty, most magnificent name of Jesus I pray, AMEN!

Notes

Write your daily inspiring prayer, scriptures, thoughts, etc.

Day 1

_____

_____

_____

_____

_____

_____

_____

_____

_____

_____

_____

_____

_____

_____

_____

_____

_____

_____

_____

_____

_____

_____

_____

_____

_____

_____

_____

Day 2

_____
_____
_____
_____
_____
_____
_____
_____
_____
_____
_____
_____
_____
_____
_____
_____
_____
_____
_____
_____
_____
_____
_____
_____
_____
_____
_____
_____

Day 3

Day 4

Day 5

_____
_____
_____
_____
_____
_____
_____
_____
_____
_____
_____
_____
_____
_____
_____
_____
_____
_____
_____
_____
_____
_____
_____
_____
_____
_____
_____
_____

Day 6

_____
_____
_____
_____
_____
_____
_____
_____
_____
_____
_____
_____
_____
_____
_____
_____
_____
_____
_____
_____
_____
_____
_____
_____
_____
_____
_____
_____
_____
_____
_____
_____
_____

Day 7

_____
_____
_____
_____
_____
_____
_____
_____
_____
_____
_____
_____
_____
_____
_____
_____
_____
_____
_____
_____
_____
_____
_____
_____
_____
_____
_____
_____
_____

Day 8

_____
_____
_____
_____
_____
_____
_____
_____
_____
_____
_____
_____
_____
_____
_____
_____
_____
_____
_____
_____
_____
_____
_____
_____
_____
_____
_____
_____
_____
_____

Day 9

_____
_____
_____
_____
_____
_____
_____
_____
_____
_____
_____
_____
_____
_____
_____
_____
_____
_____
_____
_____
_____
_____
_____
_____
_____
_____
_____
_____
_____
_____
_____
_____

Day 10

_____
_____
_____
_____
_____
_____
_____
_____
_____
_____
_____
_____
_____
_____
_____
_____
_____
_____
_____
_____
_____
_____
_____
_____
_____
_____
_____
_____
_____

Day 11

_____
_____
_____
_____
_____
_____
_____
_____
_____
_____
_____
_____
_____
_____
_____
_____
_____
_____
_____
_____
_____
_____
_____
_____
_____
_____
_____
_____

Day 12

Day 13

_____
_____
_____
_____
_____
_____
_____
_____
_____
_____
_____
_____
_____
_____
_____
_____
_____
_____
_____
_____
_____
_____
_____
_____
_____
_____
_____
_____

Day 14

Day 15

Day 16

_____
_____
_____
_____
_____
_____
_____
_____
_____
_____
_____
_____
_____
_____
_____
_____
_____
_____
_____
_____
_____
_____
_____
_____
_____
_____
_____

Day 17

_____
_____
_____
_____
_____
_____
_____
_____
_____
_____
_____
_____
_____
_____
_____
_____
_____
_____
_____
_____
_____
_____
_____
_____
_____
_____
_____
_____
_____
_____

Day 18

Day 19

_____
_____
_____
_____
_____
_____
_____
_____
_____
_____
_____
_____
_____
_____
_____
_____
_____
_____
_____
_____
_____
_____
_____
_____
_____
_____
_____
_____
_____

Inspirational Message

Topic: God is working

Scripture: I am convinced and confident of this very thing, that He who has begun a good work in you will [continue to] perfect and complete it until the day of Christ Jesus [the time of His return]. Philippians 1:6 (AMP)

In conclusion, I want you to be encouraged in your struggles knowing that God is working on your behalf! Through the good and the bad, God is doing great things behind the scenes! He is using the imperfections of life to perfect you! The flaws and the short comings of your life, if you would just entrust them into his hands; HE will work them out for your good!

The thing I love about this text; it shows the consistency of God. He won't start a perfect work only to leave it in the hands of an imperfect people. Rather, it says HE that begun the work, HE is going to perform it, HE is going to complete it, HE is going to perfect it until the day of Jesus Christ! God won't open you up, only to cause contamination and infection to take over. He's there continuously working on you, working for you, and causing all the imperfection to come to a peak of perfection. Don't give up in the midst of the perfecting process.

Through your tears know he will turn your mourning into Joy. Through the hard times, know that he will deliver you and set you free. Free from the stain of sin, free from the guilt of the past. GOD IS NOT THROUGH WITH YOU!

About the Author

Cornelius W. Dixon is a young inspiring minister/author/ and singer. Cornelius' hope is to show forth the glory and praises of God through the ministries of song and writing. Through his life's experiences, he has come to know God in a deeper and more intimate way than ever before.

Not looking for money or fame; Cornelius' desire is to spread the message of Christ to the nations by way of the book writing industry. God is truly blessing the works of his hands, as Cornelius continue to open himself and avail his every asset to God for the use of his glory!

Other books written by Cornelius can be found on Amazon.com, Createspace.com/estore, and many other online retailers. Titles include:

1. Reaching Beyond The Break
2. Reaching Beyond The Break Journal
3. The Serial Killer Ministries (Pt. 1)
4. From Lo-Debar To The Mountain Top
5. WOW Moments (Vol. 1)

Made in the USA
Columbia, SC
28 February 2023